Zucchini,

Pumpkins

&

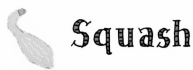 Squash

ZUCCHINI, PUMPKINS & SQUASH

KATHLEEN DESMOND STANG

Illustrated by Diane Varney

CHRONICLE BOOKS
SAN FRANCISCO

Library of Congress Cataloging-in-Publication Data:

Stang, Kathleen Desmond.
    Zucchini, pumpkins and squash/by Kathleen Desmond Stang; illustrations by Diane Varney.
      p.   cm.
    Includes index.
    ISBN 0-8118-1389-4
    1. Cookery (Squash) 2. Cookery (Pumpkin) I. Title.
    TX803.S67S73 1998
    641.6'562—dc21   96-38865
                          CIP

Printed in Hong Kong.

Designed by Vanessa Warheit at Left/Right Studio.

Distributed in Canada by
Raincoast Books
8680 Cambie Street
Vancouver, British Columbia V6P 6M9

10 9 8 7 6 5 4 3 2 1

Chronicle Books
85 Second Street
San Francisco, California 94105

Web Site: www.chronbooks.com

To my siblings,

Margaret, Eileen, Jerry, and Patricia.

And to Bob

SQUASH LOVERS ALL.

ACKNOWLEDGMENTS

Special thanks to all who helped, especially to Leslie Jonath, to Susan Derecskey, and to Dr. James R. Baggett for his help with the Glossary.

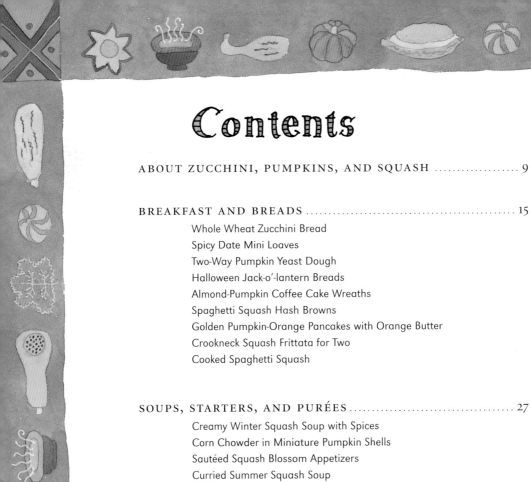

Contents

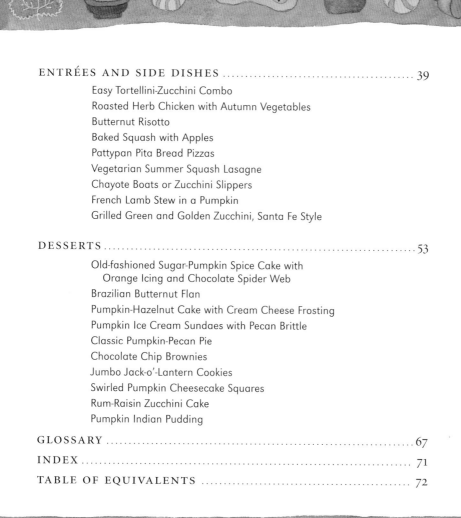

"WE HAVE PUMPKINS AT MORNING,

PUMPKINS AT NOON.

IF IT WERE NOT FOR PUMPKINS

WE SHOULD BE UNDOON."

Anonymous
(SEVENTEENTH-CENTURY NEW ENGLAND)

About Zucchini, Pumpkins, and Squash

If asked to name my favorite summer vegetable, I'd pick yellow crookneck squash any time. An old-fashioned variety, it is at its best when picked within the hour, sautéed or grilled, and sprinkled maybe with a little fresh thyme from the garden.

In winter, I'd have to vote for the creamy, rich flavor and colorful shape of the turban squash. This green, gold, and orange-splotched squash makes a spectacular fall centerpiece. That is, until it is turned into a steaming soup that fills the house with its fragrance.

On a blustery fall afternoon, though, when golden pumpkins are piled high at farm stands, my choice would be, not a giant jack-o'-lantern, the size of Cinderella's coach, with its stringy, tasteless meat, but a little sugar pumpkin, the kind to bake with maple syrup as our ancestors might have done, or to turn into a Classic Pumpkin-Pecan Pie.

SUMMER VERSUS WINTER SQUASH

Squashes and pumpkins, along with cucumbers and melons, are part of the vast gourd family known as Cucurbitaceae.

Most squashes, including pumpkins, are in the genus *Cucurbita*, which is generally subdivided into two groups: tender-skinned summer squash and hard-shelled winter squash.

The summer squashes are identified by their thin skin and mild flavor. The entire squash is edible, including the blossom, skin, and seeds. Examples include the scalloped-edge pattypan, bright yellow Sunburst, and the prolific zucchini.

This group, commonly referred to as summer squash, is picked immature, while the skin is still tender and the flavor delicate. In general, the different types can be used interchangeably in recipes. The peak season for summer squash is July through September.

Winter squash, on the other hand, is allowed to ripen to maturity. The shell hardens to protect the meaty interior and may no longer be edible. The range of winter squash includes smooth-skinned butternut with its exceptional nutty flavor and bright orange meat; elongated, green-striped Delicata; and the tiny, edible mini-pumpkins, such as Jack-Be-Little and Munchkin.

Pumpkins, those orange globes of autumn, are famous for Halloween jack-o'-lanterns and holiday pumpkin pie. But are pumpkins really any different from other squashes? Actually, no. Be they large for carving or small for baking, all pumpkins are members of the winter squash family. It may be part of our American heritage, but we like to treat pumpkins as something special.

Unlike tender summer squashes, which can be eaten raw, winter squashes must be cooked to make them palatable as well as to bring out their characteristic flavors, whether mild or bold, nutlike or sweet. The texture of winter squash ranges from coarse or fibrous to smooth and creamy. Although there are many sizes and shapes, the different varieties of winter squash can generally be used interchangeably.

Winter squash is generally planted in summer and harvested in the fall. The squash stores well in a cool, dark, dry place for several months. The peak buying season is September through February, though some varieties, with proper storage, keep well for a year.

The yellow-skinned, watermelon-shaped spaghetti squash fits somewhere between summer squash and winter squash. When cooked, the meat turns into flavorful, golden, spaghetti-like strands that are easy to scrape out of the shell with a fork. Its buying season is August through February.

For more information, see the glossary of squash varieties on page 67.

HISTORY AND LORE

The squashes and pumpkins we know today are native to the Americas. Squash was one of the earliest cultivated plants in the hemisphere. Excavations in Mexico and Peru indicate that squash dates back to 6000 to 4000 B.C.

Thousands of years ago, squash moved north, brought by migrating peoples to what is now the United States. Along with corn and beans, it became a staple of the Native American diet. The name *squash* is, in fact, derived from the Narraganset word *askutasquash.*

It was not until Columbus and the Spanish conquistadors returned from the New World, that Europeans tasted squash and pumpkin. From Europe, cultivation spread to Asia and Africa.

GROWING SQUASH

Squash is very easy to grow. It does require rich soil, plenty of sunshine and water, and lots of room, especially for the hard-shelled varieties. The squash clan is a warm season crop and will thrive in most parts of the United States. Every year, it seems, new varieties appear.

Pick summer squash straight from the garden when it is immature, tender, and flavorful. In peak season, this might be every day. When gathering squash blossoms, choose the male flowers, so the female flowers, which have tiny immature squashes at the base, will continue to fruit.

Leave hard-shelled winter squash to mature fully before harvesting. You may need to place a large squash or pumpkin on a wooden shingle to prevent the underside from rotting. Pick when the vine dies back, leaving a two- or three-inch stem. A light frost will not hurt, but bring the squash in before it gets really cold.

CHOOSING AND STORING SQUASH

Select squash carefully for maximum flavor and nutrients.

When purchasing thin-skinned summer squash, look for firm specimens, heavy for their size. Avoid any that are bruised or moldy. Summer squash will last only three or four days. Keep it, unwashed, in an unsealed bag in the crisper drawer of the refrigerator.

Winter squash, on the other hand, will last for months if properly handled. Choose specimens that are firm and heavy for their size. Avoid any with cracks or signs of decay.

Store hard-shelled squash in a well-ventilated, dark, cool, dry place for up to six months. Check occasionally, particularly on the underside, to be sure no soft spots have developed.

In supermarkets, large squash, such as banana or Hubbard, are often sold in pieces. These can be loosely wrapped and refrigerated for several days.

For longer storage, any of the hard-shelled varieties, including the small pumpkins, can be steamed, baked, or microwaved *(see page 26)* until tender, then puréed. Cover tightly and freeze for up to six months.

COOKING WITH SQUASH

The two groups of squash — the thin-skinned summer squash and the hard-shelled winter squash — are handled in entirely different ways in the kitchen.

To prepare *summer squash*, rinse the squash just before cooking, but do not peel it unless the squash is overgrown and the skin is tough. In that case, you may need to discard the seeds too. Cut off and discard the ends. Slice, dice, or julienne the squash, or leave it whole.

The many varieties of thin-skinned squash can be treated basically in the same way. Summer squash requires little or no cooking. Sliced raw squash is a good addition to crudités or on a relish tray.

Stir-frying, steaming, and microwaving are ideal cooking methods for these tender, mild squashes. Slice or dice the squash and stir-fry in a little olive or vegetable oil just until crisp-tender. Steam whole or sliced squash on a rack over boiling water, being careful not to overcook. Or microwave sliced squash tossed with minced herbs and black pepper for a fat-free vegetable dish.

Allow about four to eight ounces summer squash per serving.

To prepare *winter squash*, rinse the squash and, depending on the size and shape, cut it in half or cut off the top to form a container for stuffing. Scoop out and discard the seeds and fibers (unless you are saving the seeds to toast). Cut large squash, such as Hubbard and banana, into serving pieces.

Some squash shells are so tough they may require an ax or a hacksaw to cut them. Another possibility is to poke a few holes in the squash and then bake or microwave it to soften before cutting.

In general, all the hard-shelled squash can be cooked and used in the same way. For best results, bake winter squash in a conventional oven or microwave oven. Bake, cut side down, on a baking sheet, at 350 to 375 degrees until fork tender. Or microwave in a covered dish, cut side down, with a few spoonfuls of water on "high" (100%) for seven to ten minutes per pound. Then let stand a few minutes to finish cooking. This method may not be as flavorful as baking, but it certainly is convenient. Boiling and steaming are less successful, because the squash tends to absorb the moisture and become watery.

Season winter squash with sweet, fruity, and spicy flavors, such as maple syrup or brown sugar, diced apples or shredded orange peel, cinnamon or ginger. Or go the savory route with herbs, chilies, or just salt and freshly ground pepper.

Plan on at least six to eight ounces of winter squash per person.

NUTRITION

Squash is one of the world's most nutritious vegetables, rich in vitamins and low in fat and sodium.

Summer squash is a good source of Vitamin C. A cup of cooked zucchini yields only about 30 calories.

The firm, yellow-orange meat of winter squash and pumpkin provides an outstanding source of beta-carotene, which the body converts to Vitamin A. And one cup of cooked winter squash is just 90 to 130 calories. Spaghetti squash contains 45 calories per cup, far lower than real spaghetti.

All squashes, but particularly the winter varieties, are excellent sources of dietary fiber, which is generally lacking in the typical American diet.

And don't forget pumpkin seeds. They are rich in protein and iron. If you are growing your own pumpkins, look for a variety with hull-less seeds, such as Lady Godiva.

Luckily, squash is always available. In summer, it may be hard to keep up with the out-of-control zucchini. But soon the fields are dotted with golden pumpkins, poking out from the fading leaves. Even in winter, zucchini and acorn squash are in the supermarket produce bins. And there is always the old reliable, canned pumpkin purée, a pantry standby.

Squash, a year-round treat — for breakfast, lunch, dinner, and dessert!

Breakfast and Breads

Breakfast and Breads

Whole Wheat Zucchini Bread

Makes 1 loaf.

Use zucchini, pattypan, or crookneck, whichever summer squash is the most abundant.

1 large (8-ounce) zucchini or other
   summer squash
1 cup whole wheat flour
¾ cup all-purpose flour
1 teaspoon ground cinnamon
½ teaspoon baking soda
¼ teaspoon baking powder
½ teaspoon salt

¾ cup (packed) brown sugar
½ cup milk
¼ cup vegetable oil
1 large egg, lightly beaten
1 teaspoon grated lemon peel
½ teaspoon vanilla extract
½ cup currants or chopped walnuts

Preheat oven to 350 degrees. Position the coarse shredding disk in a food processor and shred the zucchini. You should have 1 cup.

Combine the whole wheat flour, all-purpose flour, cinnamon, baking soda, baking powder, and salt in a large bowl. Set aside.

Position the knife blade in the food processor. Place the brown sugar, milk, oil, egg, lemon peel, and vanilla in the food processor bowl. Pulse on and off until mixed. Add the shredded zucchini and currants. Pulse on and off until well mixed. Add the flour mixture and pulse on and off just until combined. Spoon into a greased 8½ x 4½ x 2½-inch loaf pan. Bake for 50 to 60 minutes, or until a wooden toothpick inserted near the center comes out clean. Cool in the pan for 10 minutes. Unmold onto a rack to cool thoroughly.

Cut into ½-inch slices to serve.

Spicy Date Mini Loaves

Makes 3 small loaves.

A perfect host or hostess gift any time of year. If you prefer, you can make one large, nine-inch loaf; bake it for 60 to 65 minutes.

1 cup all-purpose flour
⅔ cup whole wheat flour
1 teaspoon baking soda
1 teaspoon ground cinnamon
½ teaspoon ground cloves
¼ teaspoon ground allspice
¼ teaspoon salt
1¼ cups pumpkin or winter squash purée,
  canned or homemade *(see page 36)*

½ cup (packed) brown sugar
1 egg, slightly beaten
¼ cup plain lowfat yogurt
2 tablespoons vegetable oil
½ cup chopped dates
1 tablespoon hulled pumpkin seeds
  or pine nuts

Preheat oven to 350 degrees. Combine the flour, the whole wheat flour, baking soda, cinnamon, cloves, allspice, and salt in a large bowl. Set aside.

Combine the pumpkin purée, brown sugar, egg, yogurt, oil, and dates in a large bowl. Add the flour mixture and stir just until moistened.

Spoon into 3 greased 5¾ x 3¼ x 2-inch loaf pans. Sprinkle with pumpkin seeds. Bake for 35 to 40 minutes, or until a wooden toothpick inserted near the center comes out clean. Cool in the pan for 5 minutes. Unmold onto a rack to cool thoroughly.

Cut into thin slices to serve.

Two-Way Pumpkin Yeast Dough

Makes 4 Halloween Breads or 2 Coffee Cake Wreaths.

Kids will have fun with this easy-to-work-with yeast dough. Shape into Halloween pumpkin breads or, with the help of an adult, almond-filled wreaths.

6¼ to 6¾ cups all-purpose flour
¾ cup (packed) light brown sugar
2 packages fast-rising yeast
1 teaspoon salt
1 teaspoon ground cinnamon
½ teaspoon ground nutmeg

1¼ cups milk
4 tablespoons (½ stick) butter
1 cup pumpkin or winter squash purée, canned or homemade *(see page 36)*
3 large eggs, slightly beaten
1 teaspoon vanilla extract

Combine 3 cups of the flour, the brown sugar, yeast, salt, cinnamon, and nutmeg in the large bowl of an electric mixer. Heat the milk and butter in a saucepan or microwave to 120 to 130 degrees. Pour over the flour mixture and beat for 1 minute. Add the pumpkin purée, eggs, and vanilla and beat for 2 minutes more at medium speed. Gradually stir in enough of the remaining flour to make a soft dough. Knead with a dough hook or by hand on a floured surface until smooth and elastic. Place in an oiled bowl, cover, and let rise in a warm place until doubled, about 1 hour.

Punch down the dough and knead briefly on a floured surface.

To continue, see Halloween Jack-o'-lantern Breads *(page 19)* or Almond-Pumpkin Coffee Cake Wreaths *(page 21)*.

NOTE: *At this point, half or all of the dough can be placed in a plastic bag and refrigerated for up to 24 hours. Bring to room temperature before continuing.*

Halloween Jack-o'-lantern Breads

Makes 4 breads.

This bread is particularly good toasted and spread with orange marmalade.

1 recipe Two-Way Pumpkin Yeast Dough
  (page 18)
Currants, for decoration

1 egg white, beaten with 2 teaspoons water
Cinnamon sugar *(optional)*

Divide the dough into 4 equal pieces. Cover and let rest for 5 to 10 minutes.

Use 1 piece of the dough for each Jack-o'-lantern. Pinch off a small knob of dough and shape into a pumpkin stem. Shape the remaining dough into a ball and flatten to make a pumpkin shape about 9 x 7 inches. Place on greased baking sheet touching the stem, so that the two pieces will connect while baking. Make shallow cuts to resemble a pumpkin and decorate with currants as desired. Cover with a towel and repeat with remaining dough. Let the breads rise in a warm place until almost doubled, about 30 minutes.

Preheat oven to 350 degrees. Brush breads with egg white and water mixture. Sprinkle with cinnamon sugar, if desired. Bake for 30 minutes, or until golden brown. Cool for 10 minutes on a rack.

Serve warm or cool completely.

Almond-Pumpkin Coffee Cake Wreaths

Makes 2 wreaths.

Serve one coffee cake hot from the oven. Wrap and freeze the second one for another time.

1 recipe Two-Way Pumpkin Yeast Dough
  (page 18)
1 can (8 ounces) almond paste, crumbled
4 tablespoons butter (½ stick), softened
¼ cup (packed) light brown sugar

2 tablespoons all-purpose flour
½ teaspoon ground cinnamon
1 egg yolk, beaten with 1 tablespoon water
¼ cup sliced almonds

Divide the dough into 2 equal parts. Cover and let rest for 10 minutes.

Combine the almond paste, butter, brown sugar, flour, and cinnamon in a bowl. Set aside. Roll out 1 piece of dough to a 24 x 9-inch rectangle on a lightly floured surface. Sprinkle with half of the almond paste mixture. From the long side, roll up loosely, jelly-roll fashion. Transfer the roll, seam side down, to a large greased baking sheet and press together ends to form a ring. Using kitchen shears or a sharp knife, make ½-inch cuts, three quarters of the way through along the outer edge of the ring. Turn the cuts on an angle to expose the filling. Repeat for the second ring. Cover and let rise in a warm place until puffy, about 30 minutes.

Preheat oven to 350 degrees. Brush the rings with egg wash and sprinkle with almonds. Brush again with egg wash. Bake for 30 to 35 minutes, or until golden brown. Transfer to a rack.

Serve warm or at room temperature.

Spaghetti Squash Hash Browns

Makes 4 servings.

A great take on an American classic — glorious, golden comfort food. Try these easy hash browns for breakfast, dinner, or even a midnight snack.

4 to 5 cups (packed) cooked and shredded spaghetti squash *(see page 26)*

2 to 4 tablespoons finely chopped onion

2 to 3 tablespoons shredded Monterey Jack or Parmesan cheese *(optional)*

2 tablespoons all-purpose flour

¼ teaspoon salt

¼ teaspoon freshly ground black pepper

1 to 3 tablespoons butter, olive oil, or bacon drippings

1 teaspoon minced fresh chives or parsley *(optional)*

Combine the spaghetti squash, onion, cheese (if using), flour, salt, and pepper in a large bowl. Heat the butter in a large skillet over medium heat. Add the squash mixture to the pan and pat into a cake. Cook, shaking the pan occasionally to prevent sticking, until the bottom is crisp and brown, about 10 minutes. Cut into quarters and turn over. Continue cooking until the bottom is crisp and brown, about 5 to 10 minutes longer.

Serve on warm plates and sprinkle with chives, if desired.

Golden Pumpkin-Orange Pancakes with Orange Butter

Makes about 24 three-inch pancakes.

If the pancake batter seems a little too thick, my husband, the pancake pro, suggests adding a little more orange juice. These are good with maple syrup too.

1 large egg

½ cup buttermilk

½ cup pumpkin or winter squash purée, canned or homemade *(see page 36)*

1 teaspoon grated orange peel

½ cup orange juice

1 tablespoon oil or melted butter

⅔ cup all-purpose flour

⅔ cup yellow cornmeal

2 tablespoons sugar

2 teaspoons baking powder

½ teaspoon salt

Vegetable oil

Orange Butter *(recipe follows)*

ORANGE BUTTER

Makes about ½ cup.

4 tablespoons (½ stick) butter, softened

1 cup (unsifted) confectioners' sugar

2 teaspoons grated orange peel

Whisk together the egg, buttermilk, pumpkin purée, orange peel, orange juice, and oil in a large bowl. Combine the flour, cornmeal, sugar, baking powder, and salt in a separate bowl. Add to the pumpkin mixture and stir until blended.

Heat a griddle over medium heat. Brush lightly with oil. Spoon a generous tablespoon of batter per pancake onto the griddle. Cook about 2 minutes on each side, or until browned and cooked through. Continue with remaining batter. Serve the pancakes warm with Orange Butter *(see below)*.

TO MAKE THE ORANGE BUTTER: Combine the butter, confectioners' sugar, and orange peel in a bowl. Beat until smooth. Serve at room temperature.

NOTE: *The Orange Butter can be made ahead and refrigerated. Bring to room temperature before serving.*

Crookneck Squash Frittata for Two

Makes 2 generous servings.

Serve this frittata for breakfast, brunch, or a simple dinner. You might have most of these ingredients in your summer garden. Garnish with cherry tomatoes or with salsa.

2 teaspoons olive oil

2 tablespoons chopped onion or sliced green onions

¼ pound mushrooms, thinly sliced

1 medium crookneck squash or zucchini, thinly sliced

1 cup chopped tender chard leaves or spinach

1 tablespoon minced fresh parsley

½ teaspoon minced fresh basil or oregano

Salt and freshly ground black pepper, to taste

3 large eggs, lightly beaten with 2 teaspoons water

2 to 3 tablespoons shredded Gruyère or Parmesan cheese

Heat the olive oil in a 10-inch nonstick skillet over medium-high heat. Add the onion and mushrooms and sauté for 2 minutes. Add the squash, chard, parsley, basil, salt, and pepper. Sauté for about 2 minutes, or until the vegetables are crisp-tender. Pour in the eggs, cover and cook for about 2 minutes, or until eggs are almost set.

If you have a broilerproof skillet, sprinkle the frittata with cheese and broil until set. If not, position a plate over the skillet and turn over. Slide the frittata, cooked side up, back into the skillet. Sprinkle with cheese, cover, and cook for 1 or 2 minutes more, or until the cheese melts.

Cut into wedges and serve warm or at room temperature.

Cooked Spaghetti Squash

Makes 4 to 5 cups.

Serve a pasta sauce over cooked spaghetti squash for an easy and healthful meal.

1 medium (3 pounds) spaghetti squash

Cut the squash lengthwise in half and scrape out the seeds. Pierce the skin several times with a kitchen fork.

OVEN DIRECTIONS: Preheat the oven to 350 degrees. Place the squash, cut side down, in a large baking dish. Bake for 50 to 70 minutes, or until the strands can be easily scraped from the shell with a table fork.

MICROWAVE DIRECTIONS: Place one half of the squash, cut side up, in a large microwave-safe dish or on a paper towel. Microwave at "high" (100%), rotating the dish once, for about 15 minutes, or until the strands can be easily scraped from the shell with a table fork. Repeat with the remaining half.

NOTE: *Cooked spaghetti squash can be refrigerated, covered, for 1 to 2 days.*

Soups, Starters, and Purées

Soups, Starters, and Purées

Creamy Winter Squash Soup with Spices

Makes 8 to 10 servings.

Walter Bronowitz, Chef-Instructor at Edmonds Community College, makes a huge pot of this mixed squash soup every year at Seattle's Pike Place Market Labor Day Festival. He explains how to "temper" the soup to prevent it from curdling.

4 pounds assorted winter squash, such as turban, Hubbard, or Australian Blue
1 tablespoon ground cumin
1 tablespoon ground coriander
2 teaspoons minced fresh sage or ¾ teaspoon dried rubbed sage
1½ teaspoons ground mace
3 tablespoons olive oil
1½ tablespoons minced fresh hot chile, such as jalapeño

1 large onion, finely chopped
1 tart apple, such as Gravenstein or Granny Smith, peeled and grated
6 cups chicken or vegetable broth
Salt and freshly ground black pepper, to taste
1 cup cream, sour cream, or plain yogurt
Croutons, fresh sage leaves, or whipped cream, for garnish *(optional)*

Preheat oven to 375 degrees. Cut the squashes in half and scoop out the seeds and fibers. Place, cut side down, on a large, shallow baking pan. Bake for 45 minutes to 1¼ hours, or until very soft. Let cool, then scrape the squash meat from the skin. Discard the skin and mash the squash. Set aside.

While the squash is baking, combine the cumin and coriander in a dry sauté pan. Toast, stirring constantly, until the spices change color and begin to smoke. Immediately remove from the pan and let cool. Add the sage and mace.

Heat the olive oil in a large heavy saucepan over medium heat. Add the chiles and sauté for 5 minutes. Add the onion, partially cover, and continue to cook, stirring occasionally, until soft but not brown, about 5 minutes. Stir in the spice mixture. Add the apple to the pan. Increase the heat and cook, uncovered, stirring until the apple mixture becomes dry and begins to brown. Add the broth and scrape up the ingredients from the bottom of the pan with a wooden spoon. Stir in the mashed squash, bring to a simmer, and cook for 30 minutes. Purée the soup in a blender or food processor in several batches. Strain the soup, if desired. Season with salt and pepper. (Refrigerate or freeze soup at this point, if desired. Reheat if necessary.)

Place the cream, sour cream, or yogurt in a large bowl and gradually whisk in 1 cup of the hot soup. Then whisk in 2 more cups of the hot soup. Continue adding the hot soup until the outside of the bowl feels hot. Transfer the contents of the bowl back to the pan.

Serve immediately or keep warm over low heat. Do not boil. Garnish with croutons, fresh sage leaves, or whipped cream, if desired.

NOTE: *Wear rubber gloves when chopping chiles.*

Corn Chowder in Miniature Pumpkin Shells

Makes 4 servings.

Whimsical little pumpkins filled with a cream soup make a perfect starter on Thanksgiving.

4 mini-pumpkins or Carnival, Sweet
    Dumpling, or acorn squashes
    (¾ to 1¼ pounds each)
1 slice bacon, diced
¼ cup finely chopped onion
1 tablespoon all-purpose flour

½ teaspoon chili powder
1 cup chicken broth
Boiling water
1 cup corn kernels
¾ cup milk
Flat-leaf parsley leaves, for garnish *(optional)*

With a small sharp knife, cut wide tops out of the pumpkins to make bowl-shaped shells. Scrape out and discard seeds and stringy pulp. Trim all but ¼ inch of meat from tops. Using a knife and soup spoon, cut and scrape out some of the pumpkin meat, leaving a ⅜-inch-thick shell. (Shells should have about a ¾-cup capacity.) Chop the pumpkin meat and set aside.

MICROWAVE DIRECTIONS: Place the bacon in a 2-quart microwave-safe dish. Microwave at "high" (100%) for 1 minute and 45 seconds to 2 minutes, or until crisp, stirring twice. Remove the bacon and set aside. Add the onion and chopped pumpkin meat to the dish. Cover with the lid or vented heavy-duty plastic wrap and microwave at "high" for 2 minutes, or until soft. Stir in the flour and chili powder, then the chicken broth. Microwave, covered, at "high" for 5 minutes, or until the pumpkin is very soft. Meanwhile, pour boiling water into the pumpkin shells to warm them. Mash the pumpkin mixture with a fork to a coarse purée. Add the corn and milk. Microwave at "high" for 1 to 2 minutes, or until thoroughly heated.

STOVE-TOP DIRECTIONS: Sauté the bacon in a saucepan for 3 minutes, or until crisp. Remove the bacon and set aside. Add the onion and chopped pumpkin meat to the saucepan. Sauté over medium heat until tender, about 10 minutes. Stir in the flour and chili powder, then the chicken broth. Cook for 5 minutes more, or until the pumpkin is very soft. Meanwhile, pour boiling water into the pumpkin shells to warm them. Mash the pumpkin mixture with a fork to a coarse purée. Add the corn and milk. Continue to cook until thoroughly heated.

Empty and dry the pumpkin shells. Fill with the chowder. Sprinkle the bacon on top and garnish with parsley, if desired. Serve at once.

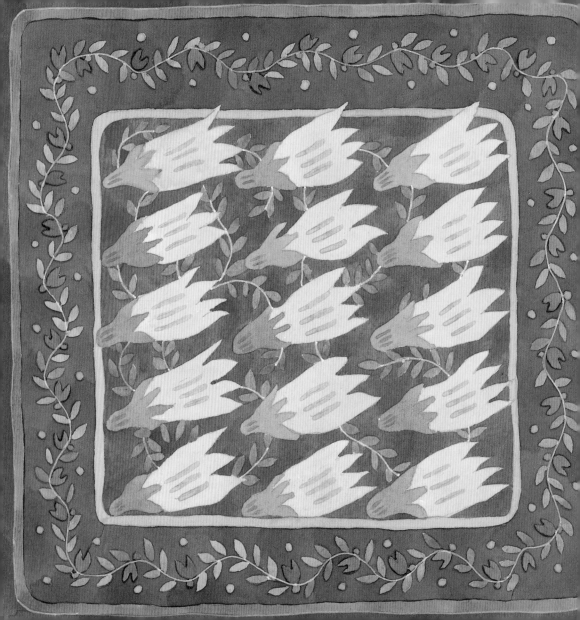

Sautéed Squash Blossom Appetizers

Makes 12 appetizers.

I am indebted to the mother of Chronicle Books editor Leslie Jonath for this sophisticated recipe. It calls for three herbs that thrive in most summer gardens.

12 large squash blossoms
2 tablespoons finely chopped fresh basil
2 tablespoons finely chopped fresh flat-leaf parsley
1 tablespoon finely chopped fresh chives or green onion
½ teaspoon freshly ground black pepper
8 ounces fresh mozzarella, cut into 12 fingers (1 x ½ x ½ inch)

1 egg or 2 eggs if blossoms are very large, lightly beaten
2 teaspoons water
⅛ teaspoon salt, or to taste
½ cup all-purpose flour
2 to 3 tablespoons olive oil
Lemon wedges, for serving *(optional)*

Remove and discard the stems from the squash blossoms. Set aside the blossoms. Combine the basil, parsley, chives, and pepper in a shallow dish. Coat each cheese finger with the herb mixture and place in a squash blossom. Twist to close. Combine the egg, 2 teaspoons water, and salt in a shallow dish. Coat the blossoms with the egg mixture, then roll in the flour. Place on a tray. Blossoms can be refrigerated, covered, for up to 2 hours.

Heat the oil in a large skillet over medium-high heat. Add as many blossoms to the skillet as fit easily. Cook, turning occasionally, for 3 to 5 minutes, or until golden brown. Drain on paper towels. Place in a low oven until all are cooked.

Serve warm, with lemon wedges, if desired.

Curried Summer Squash Soup

Makes 6 servings.

Greg Atkinson, chef at Friday Harbor House on San Juan Island, Washington, suggests this robust soup with Indian flavors as a great use for those inevitable overgrown summer squash.

Garam masala, a blend of spices, varies considerably in strength. You can substitute a mixture of equal parts (half a teaspoon each) ground cardamom, coriander, cumin, and allspice.

4 tablespoons (½ stick) butter
1 medium onion, thinly sliced
1½ to 2 teaspoons garam masala
2 teaspoons curry powder
4 cups or 2 cans (14¼ ounces each) chicken broth

4 cups sliced crookneck or other summer squash (about 1½ pounds)
½ cup plain yogurt or sour cream
¼ cup toasted pistachios or almonds, chopped

Heat the butter in a skillet over medium heat. Add the onion and sauté for 10 minutes, or until golden brown. Stir in the garam masala and curry powder and cook for 1 minute more. Stir in the broth and squash and bring the mixture to a boil. Reduce the heat to low and cook for 10 minutes, or until squash is tender. Transfer a third of the soup to a food processor or blender and purée until smooth. Repeat twice with the remaining soup. If necessary, reheat the soup.

Serve hot with dollops of yogurt and a sprinkle of chopped pistachios.

Winter Squash Ravioli

Makes 24 ravioli, 4 to 6 servings.

One Christmas we were lucky enough to stay and eat at Da Bebbe Sello in Cortina d'Ampezzo, Italy. These ravioli are a simplified version of what we were served. Wonton wrappers are a real labor- and time-saver, as is a two-part pasta cooker with a drainer that lifts out of the pot.

¼ cup hazelnuts

½ cup butternut, kabocha, banana, or other winter squash purée, canned or homemade *(see page 36)*

½ cup lowfat ricotta cheese

¼ teaspoon freshly ground black pepper

⅛ teaspoon salt

Dash of nutmeg, preferably freshly grated

¼ to ½ teaspoon finely minced fresh sage leaves *(optional)*

24 (3 x 3-inch) wonton skins, thawed if necessary

Cornmeal

3 tablespoons butter

Minced fresh parsley

Freshly grated Parmesan cheese

Preheat oven to 350 degrees. Toast the hazelnuts for 10 minutes, shaking occasionally. Let cool. Chop fine and set aside.

Combine the squash purée, ricotta, pepper, salt, nutmeg, and sage (if using) in a medium bowl. Drop a rounded teaspoon of the squash mixture onto each of 4 wonton skins. With your finger, lightly moisten 2 edges of each wonton skin with water. Fold into a triangle and press to seal. Continue with the remaining wonton skins and filling. Layer between sheets of wax paper sprinkled with cornmeal.

Bring a large pot of salted water to a boil. Cook the ravioli, twelve at a time, for about 3 minutes, or until the ravioli begin to look transparent. Carefully lift from the water and drain.

As the ravioli cook, heat 1 tablespoon of the butter in a skillet. Add the first batch of drained ravioli and sauté for 2 to 3 minutes. Arrange the ravioli on a warmed platter or on plates. Cover and keep warm. Repeat with the remaining ravioli. Heat the remaining butter in the skillet. Add the hazelnuts and heat briefly.

Sprinkle the nuts and then the parsley over the ravioli. Serve with Parmesan cheese.

Two-Way Winter Squash Purée

Makes about 2 cups purée.

It is easier to bake a large squash or pumpkin in the oven. A small two-pound pumpkin, however, cooks faster in a microwave oven. Homemade purées tend to be bright yellow-orange, rather than the orange color of most canned pumpkin. Each squash has its own unique flavor.

About 2 pounds butternut or acorn squash or small sugar pumpkin

Cut the squash in half and scrape out the seeds and fibers.

OVEN DIRECTIONS: Preheat oven to 350 degrees. Place the squash, cut side down, on a large, shallow baking pan. Bake, uncovered, for 50 to 70 minutes, or until the squash is fork tender. Let cool.

MICROWAVE DIRECTIONS: Cut the squash halves into 1-inch slices or ¼-pound chunks. Peel if desired. Place, cut side down, in a microwave-safe dish. Cover with the lid or vented heavy-duty plastic wrap. Microwave at "high" (100%), for 15 minutes, or until the meat is fork tender, rearranging the squash once. In general, allow 7 to 10 minutes microwaving time per pound. Let cool.

TO MAKE THE PURÉE: Drain off any liquid and scoop the pulp from the skins. Purée the pulp in a food processor or blender, pulsing on and off until smooth. Or mash thoroughly with a potato masher or pass through a food mill. Place the purée in a strainer and allow it to drain for at least 30 minutes, or until it is as thick as canned purée or mashed potatoes. (Purée can be refrigerated, covered, for up to 2 days or frozen, well wrapped, for several months. The most convenient size container is ½ cup.)

NOTE: *A 4 ½-pound pumpkin or winter squash yields about 4 cups purée.*

Spaghetti Squash with Mushroom Sauce

Makes 4 appetizer or 2 entrée servings.

If you miss the chanterelle or porcini season, commercially grown portobellos and cremini are available year-round. Serve with a crusty bread. The recipe can be doubled by using two skillets or a very large one.

½ medium (3 to 4 pound) spaghetti squash,
cut lengthwise

2 tablespoons butter

1 tablespoon olive oil

¼ cup finely chopped shallots

2 large portobello mushrooms, stems
removed and reserved for another use,
sliced ½ inch thick and each slice halved

4 large cremini or white button mushrooms,
sliced ¼ inch thick

⅓ cup dry white wine

2 tablespoons minced fresh flat-leaf parsley

⅛ teaspoon fresh thyme leaves

¼ cup heavy cream

Salt and freshly ground black pepper,
to taste

Cook the spaghetti squash according to the directions on page 26 and keep warm.

Heat the butter and oil in a large skillet over medium heat. Add the shallots and sauté for about 5 minutes, or until golden. Add the mushrooms and sauté about 5 minutes more, or until soft. Stir in the wine and cook until the liquid is reduced to about 3 tablespoons. Stir in the parsley and thyme. Add the cream and heat until warmed through. Season with salt and pepper.

Spoon the mushroom sauce over the hot spaghetti squash. Serve warm.

Entrées and Side Dishes

Entrées and Side Dishes

Easy Tortellini-Zucchini Combo

Makes 2 servings.

A super simple dinner that can be put together just about anywhere. It's great for camping, as nothing really requires refrigeration.

4 ounces (½ package) dried cheese-filled tortellini

1 or 2 teaspoons olive oil

1 small onion, halved and thinly sliced

2 medium or 1 large zucchini, halved lengthwise if large and sliced ¼ inch thick (½ pound)

4 to 6 mushrooms, sliced

½ teaspoon dried basil, crushed

Salt and freshly ground black pepper, to taste

Shredded Parmesan cheese

Bring a large saucepan of salted water to a boil. Add the tortellini and boil for 15 to 25 minutes, or until tender.

Meanwhile, heat the olive oil in a skillet over medium-high heat. Add the onion and sauté for about 2 minutes. Add the zucchini and sauté for 3 to 5 minutes, or until lightly browned. Add the mushrooms and continue to cook for 3 to 5 minutes, or until vegetables are tender. Season with basil, salt, and pepper. Reduce the heat to low until the pasta is done.

Drain the pasta, but not too thoroughly, and add the pasta to the skillet. Heat through. Serve with Parmesan cheese.

NOTE: *It takes a lot longer at high altitudes for the pasta to cook.*

Roasted Herb Chicken with Autumn Vegetables

Makes 4 or 5 servings.

Whenever I get a chance to go home, I ask for Mom's roast chicken. It doesn't take her long to put the dish together, using the vegetables on hand. Then she's back to her true vocation, gardening.

1 whole frying chicken (3½ to 4 pounds)
8 to 10 fresh sage leaves or ¼ teaspoon dried sage
2 tablespoons olive oil
1 tablespoon red wine vinegar
1 teaspoon Dijon mustard
1½ teaspoons minced fresh thyme or ½ teaspoon dried thyme
1½ teaspoons minced fresh oregano or ½ teaspoon dried oregano

1½ pounds Hubbard, banana, turban, buttercup, calabaza, and/or other winter squash, seeded, rind removed, and meat sliced into 2 x ½-inch strips
12 to 15 small new potatoes, scrubbed, or about 1¼ pounds large potatoes, scrubbed and cut into 1-inch chunks
1 large onion, cut into wedges
Sprigs of fresh sage, thyme, and/or oregano, for garnish (*optional*)

Preheat oven to 375 degrees. Remove the chicken neck and giblets. Loosen the skin from the breast with your fingers and insert the sage leaves under the skin or sprinkle dried sage under the skin.

Combine the oil, vinegar, mustard, thyme, and oregano in a large bowl. Rub some of the mixture on the chicken. Place chicken, breast side down, in a large, shallow roasting pan. Coat the vegetables with the remaining herb mixture and arrange in the roasting pan.

Roast for 30 minutes. Turn the chicken over and stir the vegetables. Continue to cook for about 45 minutes more, or until an instant-read thermometer inserted in the thickest part of the thigh reads 185 degrees, the meat near the thigh bone is no longer pink, and the vegetables are tender.

Transfer the chicken to a large platter and surround with the vegetables. Garnish with herbs, if desired. Carve and serve.

Butternut Risotto

Makes 4 to 6 servings.

To me, risotto is food for the soul. I prefer butternut squash for its subtle, nutty flavor, but other winter squash can be used.

1 can (14½ ounces) chicken broth or 2 cups homemade broth

3 cups water

2 or 3 tablespoons olive oil

¼ cup finely chopped onion

3 cups shredded butternut or other winter squash

1 cup Arborio rice

½ cup dry white wine

¼ cup freshly grated Parmesan cheese

Salt and freshly ground black pepper, to taste

Heat the chicken broth and water in a saucepan to a slow simmer.

Heat the olive oil in a heavy saucepan over medium-high heat. Add the onion and cook until translucent, about 5 minutes. Add the shredded squash and cook over medium heat, stirring frequently, until lightly browned, 10 to 15 minutes. Add the rice and cook 1 minute, stirring constantly with a wooden spatula or spoon. Add the wine and cook and stir until the liquid has evaporated. Add ½ cup of the broth mixture and cook, stirring constantly, until the liquid is absorbed. Continue stirring in the liquid, ½ cup at a time, until all or most of the liquid has been absorbed and the rice is tender but still al dente, 20 to 25 minutes. Stir in 2 tablespoons of the Parmesan. Season with salt and pepper.

Sprinkle the remaining Parmesan on top and serve.

NOTE: *Serve the risotto as a first course, as in Italy, or as a side dish.*

Baked Squash with Apples

Makes 4 servings.

Choose any variety of the many small squashes now available. Cut them in half vertically or horizontally, whichever balances better.

2 medium (about 1½ pounds each) Carnival, acorn, Delicata, Sugar Loaf, or Gold Nugget squash

1 tablespoon butter, melted

¼ teaspoon ground allspice

2 Golden Delicious or other cooking apples, peeled, cored, cut into eighths, and sliced crosswise ¼ inch thick

2 tablespoons currants *(optional)*

2 tablespoons (packed) brown sugar

½ teaspoon ground cinnamon

Preheat oven to 400 degrees. Cut the squashes in half *(see Note)* and discard the seeds and fibers. Brush the squash cavities with a little melted butter and sprinkle with allspice. Place, cut side down, in a large shallow baking pan. Bake 30 minutes.

Meanwhile combine the apples, currants (if using), brown sugar, cinnamon, and the remaining butter. Turn the squash cut side up and divide the apple mixture among the halves. Bake for 30 minutes more, or until the squash is very tender. Serve warm.

NOTE: *You might find it easier to bake the Gold Nugget squash whole for 30 minutes before cutting.*

Pattypan Pita Bread Pizzas

Makes 4 small pizzas.

Looking for a quick lunch, a late supper, or a fancy hors d'oeuvre? These colorful mini-pizzas will fit the bill.

2 pita breads (6-inch size), each separated into 2 rounds

About 3 tablespoons olive oil

1 large red bell pepper, cored, seeded, and thinly sliced

1 small onion, thinly sliced

1 pound pattypan or other summer squash, trimmed and cut into ½-inch pieces

1 tablespoon minced fresh basil or 1 teaspoon dried basil

¼ teaspoon salt

¼ teaspoon pepper

½ cup ricotta cheese

6 black olives, pitted and sliced

Crushed red pepper, to taste

Preheat oven to 350 degrees. Brush the rough side of the pitas lightly with a little olive oil. Place, oiled side up, on a baking sheet and bake for 5 minutes. Set aside to cool.

Heat the remaining oil in a large skillet over medium heat. Add the red pepper and onion and sauté for 4 minutes. Add the squash, basil, salt, and pepper. Cook for 2 minutes more, or until vegetables are tender.

Preheat the broiler. Arrange the vegetables on the pitas. Dollop with ricotta and sprinkle with black olives and crushed red pepper. Broil 4 to 6 inches from the heat for about 1 minute, or until the cheese has softened, the vegetables are heated through, and the bread is crisp.

Cut into wedges to serve.

Vegetarian Summer Squash Lasagne

Makes 6 to 8 servings.

Lasagne is a year-round dish. This version started out one Christmas Eve with a special request from a vegetarian niece. It's fresh tasting and very low in fat.

2 large yellow straightneck or crookneck squash or other summer squash, trimmed and thinly sliced (about 1½ pounds)

1 tablespoon salt

TOMATO-MUSHROOM SAUCE

1 tablespoon olive oil

1 medium onion, chopped

1 red bell pepper, cored, seeded, and thinly sliced

½ pound mushrooms, thinly sliced

1 tablespoon all-purpose flour

1 can (28 ounces) crushed tomatoes in tomato purée

1 tablespoon minced fresh basil or 1 teaspoon dried basil

2 teaspoons minced fresh oregano or ½ teaspoon dried oregano

Salt and freshly ground black pepper, to taste

CHEESE FILLING

About 2 cups (15-ounce carton) low-fat ricotta cheese

1 package (10 ounces) frozen chopped spinach, thawed and squeezed dry

2 tablespoons chopped fresh flat-leaf parsley

4 ounces part–skim milk mozzarella cheese, thinly sliced

2 tablespoons grated Parmesan cheese

Spread the sliced squash in a large shallow dish. Sprinkle evenly with salt and let stand for about 25 minutes, turning occasionally. Rinse thoroughly in a colander and pat dry with a towel. Set aside.

TO MAKE THE SAUCE: Heat the olive oil in a large skillet over medium heat. Add the onion and red pepper and sauté until the onion is golden, about 7 minutes. Stir in the mushrooms and continue to cook for 5 minutes more. Add the flour and mix well. Stir in the tomatoes, basil, and oregano. Season with salt and pepper. Bring to a boil, reduce the heat, and simmer uncovered for 20 minutes, or until slightly thickened. Set aside. (Makes about 5 cups of sauce.)

TO MAKE THE FILLING: Combine the ricotta, spinach, and parsley. Set aside.

Preheat oven to 375 degrees. Spread a fourth of the tomato-mushroom sauce in a 13 x 9 x 2-inch baking dish. Arrange a third of the squash evenly over the sauce. Dollop with half of the cheese mixture. Add another fourth of the tomato sauce, another third of the squash, and the remaining cheese mixture. Cover with another fourth of the tomato sauce, the remaining squash, and the remaining tomato sauce. Bake for 20 minutes.

Arrange the mozzarella slices on top and sprinkle with the Parmesan. Continue to bake for 25 minutes more, or until the lasagne bubbles and is hot in the center.

Let stand for about 15 minutes before serving.

Chayote Boats or Zucchini Slippers

Makes 8 pieces.

The zucchini slipper idea came from Pidge Barry of Los Altos, California. I've adapted her zucchini recipe to suit the chayote. The whole vegetable is edible when cooked, including the seed.

4 chayotes (about 3 pounds) or 4 zucchini (about 2 pounds)

¾ cup shredded sharp Cheddar cheese (about 3 ounces)

¼ cup small-curd cottage cheese

1 egg, well beaten

1 tablespoon finely chopped fresh flat-leaf parsley

1 teaspoon minced fresh chives or green onion

½ teaspoon dried Italian seasoning

Salt and freshly ground black pepper, to taste

Paprika

Place chayotes in boiling salted water. Cover, reduce the heat, and simmer for 25 to 35 minutes, or until tender when pierced with the point of a knife. If using zucchini, cook in simmering water for 4 to 5 minutes, or until tender. Drain the squash and let cool.

Cut the squash in half lengthwise. For the chayote, remove and discard the seeds and seed casings. Cut with a grapefruit knife around the edge, leaving a ¼-inch shell. Be careful not to cut through the skin. Lift out the pulp and finely chop it. Squeeze dry. If using zucchini, trim the ends and scoop out the seedy pulp in the center. Finely chop the pulp and squeeze dry.

Preheat oven to 350 degrees. Oil a large baking sheet.

For either type of squash, combine the squash pulp, Cheddar cheese, cottage cheese, egg, parsley, chives, and Italian seasoning. Season with salt and pepper. Divide the filling among the squash halves, mounding as necessary. Place on the baking sheet and sprinkle with paprika. Bake, uncovered, for 10 to 15 minutes, or until heated through. Broil 4 to 5 inches from the heat for 2 to 3 minutes, or until golden brown.

Serve warm.

French Lamb Stew in a Pumpkin

Makes 6 to 8 servings.

My friend Nancy Frank, besides doing professional flower arrangements, is a terrific cook. Every fall she buys several big red-orange Rouge Vif d'Etampes pumpkins, which are shaped just like Cinderella's coach. Nancy uses them first as a centerpiece and later as a container for her flavorful lamb stew. This recipe can also be made with beef.

¼ cup all-purpose flour

¾ teaspoon dried rosemary, crumbled, or 2 teaspoons minced fresh rosemary leaves

¾ teaspoon dried thyme or 2 teaspoons fresh thyme leaves

Salt and freshly ground black pepper

2½ to 3 pounds lamb or beef stew meat, cut into 1-inch pieces

2 tablespoons olive oil

2 teaspoons sugar

¾ cup dry red wine

1 can (14½ ounces) beef broth

2 tablespoons tomato paste

1 to 2 cloves garlic, minced

1¾ to 2 pounds small red boiling potatoes, scrubbed, or large red potatoes scrubbed and cut into 1-inch dice

4 to 5 large carrots, cut diagonally into ½-inch pieces

2 cups frozen pearl onions, thawed

1 large (about 10 pounds) Rouge Vif d'Etampes pumpkin or other large squash with a 2-quart capacity

2 cups frozen petite peas, thawed

3 tablespoons minced fresh flat-leaf parsley

Sprigs of rosemary and thyme, for garnish *(optional)*

Preheat oven to 350 degrees. *(See Note.)* Combine the flour, rosemary, and thyme with ½ teaspoon salt and ¼ teaspoon pepper in a large plastic bag. Add a third of the meat and shake well. Heat about 2 teaspoons of oil in a large skillet over high heat. Add the coated meat and sauté until brown, about 4 minutes. Transfer to a large Dutch oven and repeat twice with the remaining meat and oil. Sprinkle the meat with the sugar. Cook and stir over high heat for 2 to 3 minutes, or until caramelized. Add the wine to the skillet, scraping loose any bits of meat. Pour into the Dutch oven. Add the broth, tomato paste, and garlic. Stir well. Add the potatoes, carrots, and onions. Cover and cook for 45 minutes.

Meanwhile, cut a wide top out of the pumpkin and set aside. Remove the seeds and fibers and discard. Place the hollowed-out pumpkin in a baking pan or bowl and heat in the oven.

Pour the simmering stew into the warm pumpkin. Continue to cook for about 45 minutes more, or until the meat, vegetables, and pumpkin meat are tender. Stir in the peas and cook for 5 minutes more, or until hot. Taste and adjust the seasonings. Sprinkle the parsley over the stew and garnish with fresh rosemary and thyme, if desired.

Serve in wide shallow bowls, scooping out some of the pumpkin meat with each serving.

NOTE: *You will need a large ovenproof pan or bowl, preferably round, to hold the pumpkin. If this pan and the Dutch oven containing the stew will not fit in the oven together, then start cooking the stew on top of the stove.*

Grilled Green and Gold Zucchini, Santa Fe Style

Makes 4 to 6 servings.

Katharine Kagel serves this dish at Cafe Pasqual's in Santa Fe. Make a salad from the leftovers by chopping the vegetables and tossing them with a spoonful of balsamic vinegar, a handful of black olives, and a sprinkle of toasted sesame seeds.

¼ cup olive oil

2 tablespoons balsamic vinegar

½ teaspoon minced garlic

½ teaspoon salt

½ teaspoon freshly ground black pepper

¼ teaspoon crushed red pepper

1 pound green zucchini, sliced lengthwise into ¼- to ½-inch strips

1 pound yellow zucchini, sliced lengthwise into ¼- to ½-inch strips

1 large red bell pepper, cut lengthwise into ½-inch strips

Combine the olive oil, vinegar, garlic, salt, pepper, and crushed red pepper in a large shallow dish. Add the vegetables and turn to coat. Marinate for 1 to 4 hours, turning occasionally.

Prepare the grill *(see Note)*.

Grill over medium-hot coals, 4 to 6 inches from the heat, basting and turning once, until the squash is tender and streaked with brown, about 10 minutes total.

Serve hot or at room temperature.

NOTE: *The vegetables can also be cooked under a broiler.*

Desserts

Desserts

Old-fashioned Sugar-Pumpkin Spice Cake
with Orange Icing and Chocolate Spider Web

Makes about 12 servings.

This easy-to-make sheet cake with an orange-flavored frosting will be a year-round favorite. On Halloween you might want to add a chocolate spider in a chocolate spider web.

2 cups all-purpose flour
2 teaspoons baking powder
½ teaspoon baking soda
½ teaspoon salt
1¼ teaspoons ground cinnamon
½ teaspoon ground ginger
¼ teaspoon ground allspice
¼ teaspoon ground cloves
¼ teaspoon ground nutmeg
8 tablespoons (1 stick) butter, softened
1¼ cups sugar
1 large egg and 2 egg whites or 2 whole
   large eggs
1 teaspoon vanilla extract

1 cup pumpkin or winter squash purée,
   canned or homemade *(see page 36)*
¾ cup lowfat milk
⅓ cup raisins or chocolate chips *(optional)*
Orange Icing *(recipe follows)*
1 ounce semisweet chocolate, chopped, for
   spider and web *(optional)*

ORANGE ICING
Makes about 1 cup.
4 tablespoons *(½ stick)* butter, softened
1 teaspoon grated orange peel
2 cups sifted confectioners' sugar
1½ to 2 tablespoons orange juice

Preheat oven to 350 degrees. Combine the flour, baking powder, baking soda, salt, cinnamon, ginger, allspice, cloves, and nutmeg in a large bowl. Set aside. Cream the butter in the large bowl of an electric mixer. Gradually beat in the sugar. Add the eggs, one at a time, and the vanilla. In a separate bowl, combine the pumpkin purée and milk. Add the flour mixture alternately with the pumpkin mixture to the butter mixture, starting and ending with the flour mixture, and stirring just until blended.

Stir in the raisins, if using. Spread the batter in a greased 13 x 9 x 2-inch pan. Bake for 30 minutes, or until a wooden pick inserted near the center comes out clean. Cool in the pan on a rack. Spread with Orange Icing (*see below*), while still in the pan. If desired, place the chocolate in a small sealable plastic bag. Immerse in warm water until melted. Snip off a tiny corner and pipe a chocolate spider and web onto the cake.

Cut into squares to serve.

TO MAKE THE ICING: Combine the butter, orange peel, and confectioners' sugar. Add enough orange juice to make a spreading consistency.

VIVA   BRAZIL

Brazilian Butternut Flan

Makes about 6 servings.

Clara, who lived next door to us in Rio de Janeiro, would buy a piece of squash at the outdoor market for her pudim de abobora, *or pumpkin pudding. The supermarket also stocked canned pumpkin with coconut or plain.*

1 ½ cups sugar
3 large eggs, beaten
1 ¼ cups milk, half-and-half, or canned evaporated milk
1 ¼ teaspoons vanilla extract

Dash of salt
1 cup butternut, calabaza, or other winter squash purée, canned or homemade *(see page 36)*

Place 1 cup of the sugar in a large heavy skillet over medium-high heat. Cook, without stirring, until the sugar begins to melt. Reduce the heat to low and cook and stir until it turns a golden brown. Quickly pour the caramel into a 9- or 10-inch (1-quart) deep-dish pie plate and tip to coat the bottom and sides.

Preheat oven to 350 degrees. Put water on to boil.

Beat the eggs with the remaining ½ cup sugar. Stir in the milk, vanilla, salt, and the squash purée. Strain the mixture and pour into the caramel-lined pan. Place in a large baking pan and add boiling water halfway up the side of the pie plate. Bake for 45 to 50 minutes, or until set in the center when gently shaken. Remove from the hot water and chill for at least 4 hours or overnight.

To serve, loosen the custard with the tip of a knife. Place a platter on top and quickly turn over. Hold in place until the caramel flows out.

Pumpkin-Hazelnut Cake with Cream Cheese Frosting

Makes 8 to 10 servings.

The fruit purée or applesauce replaces most of the fat in this lightened pumpkin cake. The fruit and pumpkin purées both help improve the keeping qualities of the cake.

2 large eggs

⅓ cup Lighter Bake (apple and prune purée) or applesauce

2 tablespoons vegetable oil

1 teaspoon vanilla extract

1½ cups all-purpose flour

1½ cups sugar

1 teaspoon baking soda

¼ teaspoon salt

1 teaspoon ground cinnamon

¼ teaspoon ground cloves

⅛ teaspoon ground nutmeg

1 cup pumpkin or winter squash purée, canned or homemade *(see page 36)*

½ cup chopped hazelnuts

Cream Cheese Frosting *(recipe follows)*

¼ cup sliced hazelnuts

CREAM CHEESE FROSTING

Makes about ¾ cup.

4 ounces cream cheese, softened

½ teaspoon vanilla extract

1½ cups sifted confectioners' sugar

Preheat oven to 350 degrees. Combine the eggs, Lighter Bake, oil, and vanilla in a bowl and mix well. In a separate bowl, stir together the flour, sugar, baking soda, salt, cinnamon, cloves, and nutmeg. Add to the egg mixture and beat well. Stir in the pumpkin purée and chopped hazelnuts. Pour into a greased 9 x 1½-inch round cake pan. Bake for 40 to 45 minutes, or until a wooden pick inserted near the center comes out clean. Cool for 5 minutes on a rack. Loosen edges and transfer to a serving plate. Frost the top and sides of the cake with Cream Cheese Frosting (*see below*) and garnish with sliced hazelnuts.

Cut into wedges to serve.

TO MAKE THE FROSTING: Combine the cream cheese, vanilla, and confectioners' sugar.

Pumpkin Ice Cream Sundaes with Pecan Brittle

Makes about 1¼ quarts.

Pumpkin ice cream is like a summertime pumpkin pie.

Yolks of 2 large eggs
¾ cup sugar
2 cups milk
1 cup pumpkin or winter squash purée, canned or homemade *(see page 36)*
1½ teaspoons ground cinnamon
¼ teaspoon ground cloves
½ teaspoon ground ginger
½ teaspoon ground nutmeg
Dash of salt

1 cup heavy cream
¾ teaspoon vanilla extract
Softly whipped cream *(optional)*
Pecan Brittle *(recipe follows)*

PECAN BRITTLE
Makes about 2 cups.
½ cup chopped pecans
Butter
1 cup sugar

TO MAKE THE ICE CREAM: Whisk together the egg yolks and sugar in a large bowl. Heat the milk in a large saucepan over medium-high heat until bubbles form around the edge. Slowly pour into the egg mixture, stirring constantly. Return the mixture to the saucepan. Reduce the heat to medium-low and cook, stirring, just until the mixture thickens and coats the back of a spoon. Do not overheat or the custard may curdle. In a small bowl, combine the pumpkin purée and the cinnamon, cloves, ginger, nutmeg, and salt. Stir into the custard. Strain into a bowl. Stir in the cream and vanilla. Chill thoroughly. Freeze in an ice-cream maker according to manufacturer's directions. Serve with softly whipped cream, if desired, and a sprinkle of Pecan Brittle *(see below)*.

TO MAKE THE PECAN BRITTLE: Place the pecans in a shallow pan and toast for 10 minutes, shaking the pan occasionally. Cool slightly and coarsely chop. Butter a large piece of foil. Heat the sugar in a large skillet over medium-high heat. Cook, shaking occasionally, until sugar melts and turns amber. Stir in the pecans and pour out onto the prepared foil. Cool. Break brittle into pieces, reserving a few large pieces to top the sundaes. Place the remaining brittle in a heavy-duty plastic bag and crush with a rolling pin.

Classic Pumpkin-Pecan Pie

Makes one 9- or 10-inch pie.

The best of all worlds: pumpkin pie and pecan pie layered in the same dish.

FLAKY PASTRY

1 cup all-purpose flour

¼ teaspoon salt

⅓ cup (5⅓ tablespoons) shortening or butter

3 to 3½ tablespoons ice water

PUMPKIN-PECAN FILLING

3 large eggs

1 cup pumpkin or winter squash purée, canned or homemade *(see page 36)*

½ cup granulated sugar

⅔ cup evaporated regular or lowfat milk

¼ teaspoon freshly grated nutmeg

⅓ cup maple syrup

¼ cup (packed) dark brown sugar

1 tablespoon butter, melted

½ teaspoon vanilla extract

Dash of salt

¾ cup pecan halves

TO MAKE THE PASTRY: Combine the flour and salt in a bowl. Cut in the shortening until mixture is the size of small peas. Gradually sprinkle in the water, 1 tablespoon at a time, until the mixture holds together when gathered with a fork. Press together into a disk, wrap in plastic wrap, and refrigerate for at least 20 minutes.

TO MAKE THE FILLING: Lightly beat 2 of the eggs. Stir in the pumpkin purée, granulated sugar, evaporated milk, and nutmeg. Set aside. Beat the remaining egg. Stir in the maple syrup, brown sugar, butter, vanilla, and salt. Mix well. Stir in the pecans.

Preheat oven to 425 degrees. Roll out the pastry on a lightly floured surface to an 11- to 12-inch circle. Transfer to a 9- or 10-inch pie pan. Trim the crust allowing a ½-inch overhang. Fold under the edge and flute. Place on a baking sheet and pour in the pumpkin mixture. Bake for 25 minutes.

Pour the pecan mixture over the pumpkin layer and spread evenly. Reduce the heat to 350 degrees and continue to bake for 20 minutes more, or until the filling is slightly puffed and a knife inserted near the center comes out clean. Cool on a rack.

Serve within 4 hours or refrigerate, loosely covered, for up to 1 day.

Chocolate Chip Brownies

Makes 16 squares.

Grated summer squash adds both moisture and a rich color to these lowfat chocolate brownies.

1¼ cups sugar
¼ cup vegetable oil
4 large egg whites or 2 whole large eggs
1½ teaspoons vanilla extract
1 cup all-purpose flour
⅔ cup unsweetened cocoa, preferably Dutch
  process or European style

½ teaspoon baking powder
¼ teaspoon salt
1 cup coarsely shredded crookneck or other
  summer squash
¼ cup miniature chocolate chips

Preheat oven to 350 degrees. Grease a 9-inch square baking pan.

Combine the sugar and oil in a bowl. Beat with an electric mixer until creamy. Beat in the egg whites and vanilla. In a separate bowl, stir together the flour, cocoa, baking powder, and salt. Add, in 2 parts, to the sugar mixture, beating well. Stir in the shredded squash and 2 tablespoons of the chocolate chips.

Pour the batter into the pan. Sprinkle with the remaining chocolate chips. Bake about 35 minutes, or until a wooden pick inserted near the center comes out clean. Cool completely on a rack.

Cut into squares to serve.

Jumbo Jack-o'-lantern Cookies

Makes 9 to 10 cookies.

Great fun for kids! These cookies are loaded with goodies.

½ cup all-purpose flour
½ cup whole wheat flour or additional
   all-purpose flour
½ teaspoon baking powder
¼ teaspoon baking soda
¼ teaspoon salt
1¼ teaspoons ground cinnamon
¼ teaspoon ground allspice
4 tablespoons (½ stick) butter, softened
½ cup honey
¼ cup (packed) brown sugar

1 large egg
½ teaspoon vanilla extract
½ cup pumpkin or winter squash purée,
   canned or homemade (*see page 36*)
1 cup quick-cooking oatmeal
½ cup sunflower seeds
½ cup currants
½ cup miniature chocolate chips
½ cup diced dried apricots
Currants, chocolate chips, and/or chocolate-
   covered candies, etc., for decoration

Preheat oven to 350 degrees. Grease 2 large baking sheets.

Combine the all-purpose flour, the whole wheat flour, baking powder, baking soda, salt, cinnamon, and allspice in a bowl. Set aside. Cream the butter, honey, and brown sugar in the large bowl of an electric mixer. Beat in the egg, vanilla, and pumpkin purée. (The mixture may not be smooth.) Stir in the flour mixture. Add the oatmeal, sunflower seeds, currants, chocolate chips, and apricots.

Using a ⅓ cup measure, scoop the dough onto the baking sheets. With a rubber spatula, form the dough into a 5-inch-wide pumpkin shape with a little dough on the top for a stem. Repeat with the remaining dough. Decorate with currants, chocolate chips, etc. Bake for about 20 minutes, or until firm. Cool for 5 minutes on the pans, then transfer the cookies to a rack and cool completely.

Swirled Pumpkin Cheesecake Squares

Makes 16 pieces.

Gingersnaps add pizazz to this rich-tasting dessert. Just a little bite is enough.

GINGERSNAP CRUST

About 20 gingersnaps, broken into
   large pieces

¼ cup granulated sugar

3 tablespoons butter, melted

CHEESECAKE FILLING

11 ounces (8- and 3-ounce packages)
   lowfat cream cheese, softened

⅓ cup lowfat sour cream

⅓ cup granulated sugar

1 tablespoon all-purpose flour

1 large egg

½ teaspoon vanilla extract

½ cup pumpkin or winter squash purée,
   canned or homemade *(see page 36)*

1 tablespoon (packed) brown sugar

Preheat oven to 325 degrees. Line the bottom and sides of a 9 x 9 x 2-inch square pan with foil. Grease the foil on the bottom and 1 inch up the sides of the pan.

TO MAKE THE CRUST: Process the gingersnaps in a food processor or blender until very finely chopped. You should have 1 cup crumbs. Combine the gingersnap crumbs, sugar, and butter in a small bowl. Pat into an even layer in the bottom of the pan. Bake for 7 minutes. Cool on a rack.

TO MAKE THE FILLING: Beat the cream cheese, sour cream, granulated sugar, and flour in the large bowl of an electric mixer. Add the egg and vanilla and beat until smooth. Place ¾ cup of the cream cheese mixture in a bowl and stir in the pumpkin purée and brown sugar.

Spoon the plain cream cheese mixture evenly over the crumb layer in the pan. Dollop the pumpkin mixture on top and swirl with a fork to make a decorative design. Bake for 25 minutes, or until firm in the middle when gently shaken. Cool in the pan for 1 hour. Chill thoroughly.

To serve, lift cheesecake and foil from the pan. Cut into squares and remove from the foil to a serving plate.

Rum-Raisin Zucchini Cake

Makes about 10 servings.

Shredded zucchini lends a pretty green touch, but any summer squash can be used.

CAKE

½ cup dark and/or golden raisins

1 tablespoon rum

1½ cups all-purpose flour

1 teaspoon baking powder

¼ teaspoon baking soda

¼ teaspoon salt

1 teaspoon ground cinnamon

½ teaspoon ground ginger

¼ teaspoon ground nutmeg

6 tablespoons (¾ stick) butter, softened

½ cup granulated sugar

½ cup (packed) light brown sugar

1 large egg, beaten

1½ cups coarsely grated zucchini or other summer squash

RUM GLAZE

1 cup sifted confectioners' sugar

About 2 tablespoons rum or 2 tablespoons milk plus ¼ teaspoon vanilla extract

Preheat oven to 325 degrees. Grease the bottom of 9 x 5 x 3-inch glass loaf pan. Line the bottom with wax paper.

TO MAKE THE CAKE: Combine the raisins and rum in a bowl. Let stand, stirring occasionally. Meanwhile, in another bowl, combine the flour, baking powder, baking soda, salt, cinnamon, ginger, and nutmeg. Set aside. Beat the butter, granulated sugar, and brown sugar in the large bowl of an electric mixer until well mixed. Add the egg and beat unti creamy. Stir in the zucchini and the raisin and rum mixture. (The mixture may look curdled.) Gradually add the flour mixture and beat on low speed. Spoon the batter into the pan.

Bake for 60 to 65 minutes, or until a wooden pick inserted in the center comes out clean. Cool for 10 minutes on a rack. Unmold and remove the wax paper. Cool completely.

TO MAKE THE GLAZE: Combine the confectioners' sugar and rum. Beat until smooth. Stir in a little warm water until a drizzling consistency is reached. Drizzle the glaze over the cooled cake. Let stand until the glaze hardens.

Cut into ¾-inch slices to serve.

Pumpkin Indian Pudding

Makes 4 servings.

A Boston specialty, with a nod to my New England ancestors.

2 cups whole or skim milk
⅓ cup yellow cornmeal, preferably
   stone-ground
2 tablespoons butter, cut in small pieces
¼ cup (packed) dark brown sugar
¼ teaspoon ground cinnamon
¼ teaspoon ground ginger

Dash of ground nutmeg
⅛ teaspoon salt
½ cup pumpkin or winter squash purée,
   canned or homemade (*see page 36*)
1 tablespoon molasses

Vanilla ice cream (*optional*)

Preheat oven to 275 degrees. Butter a 1-quart baking dish.

Combine the milk and cornmeal in a large heavy saucepan. Cook and stir over medium heat until the mixture is creamy, about 7 to 10 minutes. Remove from the heat. Add the butter and stir until melted. Combine the brown sugar, cinnamon, ginger, nutmeg, and salt in a small bowl. Stir into the milk mixture. Add the squash purée and molasses. Pour into the dish. Bake for 1½ hours, or until a knife inserted near the center comes out clean.

Serve warm with vanilla ice cream, if desired.

Glossary

SUMMER SQUASH

CROOKNECK AND YELLOW STRAIGHTNECK Dark to pale yellow, smooth to bumpy skin. Crookneck, an old-fashioned squash, has a curved neck; straightneck was developed for easy packing and shipping. Both are mild and delicately sweet, and can be used interchangeably. Yellow straightneck is lighter in color and fatter than yellow zucchini. Available most of the year.

PATTYPAN (SCALLOP, CYMLING) Pale green and flavorful when young, becomes white and soft inside as it gets larger. Scalloped disk shape. Sunburst is a bright yellow hybrid with a ruffled edge and buttery taste. Scallopini, dark green with a flying saucer shape, is a cross between pattypan and zucchini. Peak season is July through September.

ZUCCHINI (ITALIAN SQUASH, COURGETTE) Light to dark green to almost black, solid or striped, with a smooth skin. Gold Rush is a bright yellow, zucchini-shaped hybrid. The small green Ronde de Nice is a French heirloom zucchini, a round, firm fruit, creamy and fairly sweet. The original green varieties are available year-round.

WINTER SQUASH

ACORN (TABLE QUEEN, DANISH) Green to almost black, gold, or white skinned squash, shaped like a deeply ridged acorn. Weighs 1 to 3 pounds. Hard rind with smooth texture. Mildly sweet, sometimes bland and fibrous. Green may be the most flavorful. Available year-round.

AUSTRALIAN BLUE (QUEENSLAND BLUE) Pale blue, gray, or green skin, turns tan as it matures. A medium-large squatty pumpkin shape with deep ridges. Hard rind with sweet, bright orange meat. Keeps well.

BANANA Originated in Mexico. Pale orange to pinkish white, shaped like a 3- to 4-foot long banana. Soft rind with fine-textured, slightly sweet meat. Widely available. Frequently sold in 1- to 1½-pound chunks. Smaller blue and gray varieties, such as Banana Blue, are good quality and keep well.

BUTTERCUP Dark green with a gray-green "turban" on the blossom end, shaped like a flattened drum. Weighs 3 to 5 pounds. Soft rind with yellow-orange meat that may be dry. Very sweet, nutlike flavor.

BUTTERNUT A group of squashes with smooth, beige skin, generally cylindrical in shape with a round bulge at the blossom end. Weighs 2 to 5 pounds. Thick, dark golden meat with small seed cavity. Soft rind with mild texture. Nutty-sweet flavor. Widely available year-round.

CALABAZA (WEST INDIAN PUMPKIN) Generic name for several large round or pear-shaped squashes found throughout the Caribbean and Central and South America. Can be green with yellow stripes, tan, or orange. Hard rind with fine-grained, yellow-orange meat. Mild flavor. Available year-round in some Latin American markets. Often sold in precut chunks.

CARNIVAL Recent cross between acorn and Sweet Dumpling. Colorful horizontal and vertical orange, green, yellow, and cream colored stripes. About the same size as an acorn squash, but a rounder shape. Deep yellow, fibrous meat with large seed cavity. Sweet, earthy flavor.

DELICATA (SWEET POTATO SQUASH) Lengthwise green stripes over an ivory base, skin turns orange as it ripens. Elongated in shape. Weighs 1½ to 2 pounds. Soft rind with yellow-gold meat and creamy texture. Slightly sweet, delicate flavor.

GOLD NUGGET (GOLDEN NUGGET) Orange skin, often with a green ring around the stem, shaped like a miniature Cinderella coach. Very hard, inedible rind, grooved like a small pumpkin; smooth, bright orange meat. Sweet and moist, but bland if picked immature. Because of the hard shell, it is best to cook whole, either by microwaving or baking.

HUBBARD (GOLDEN, BLUE, GREEN WARTED, OR BABY BLUE) A group of squashes with tapered ends like spinning tops. Green, orange, tan or blue-gray, either smooth or warty. Most are large, 8 to 12 pounds or more, but some varieties, like Baby Blue, are small. Hard rind with sweet, golden meat. Rich and creamy. Difficult to cut. Keeps well. Available year-round, often sold in large pieces.

KABOCHA (JAPANESE PUMPKIN) A group of Hokkaido-type squash popular in Japan. Green or gray uneven stripes or bright orange skin, flattened round shape. Soft rind with orange meat. Rich flavor. Available most of the year.

LARGE FIELD PUMPKIN Orange skin, oval or round. Can weigh over 100 pounds. Soft rind good for carving. Orange meat often stringy. Some varieties good for cooking, most are watery with poor flavor. Generally best for jack-o'-lanterns or as serving dishes. Hard to find after Halloween. Perishable.

MINI-PUMPKIN (JACK-BE-LITTLE, MUNCHKIN) Orange skin, resembles a tiny Jack-o'-lantern. Often used as a decoration. Small, between 4 and 16 ounces. Orange meat with large seed cavity. Mildly sweet. Good size for individual serving, ideal for stuffing.

PUMPKIN (SUGAR PUMPKIN, SUGAR PIE, NEW ENGLAND PIE PUMPKIN, BABY BEAR, TRIPLE TREAT) Orange skin, oval or round. Small pie or cooking pumpkins average 5 to 6 pounds. Soft rind with thick, dense, non-stringy meat. Sweet flavor. Some varieties, such as Baby Bear, Lady Godiva, and Triple Treat, have hull-less seeds. Lumina and other white varieties are good for cooking and carving. Hard to find after Thanksgiving. Fairly perishable.

ROUGE VIF D'ETAMPES (ROUGE D'TAMPES, CINDERELLA, FRENCH PUMPKIN) Heirloom French variety. Bright red-orange color, large, deeply lobed, slightly flattened pumpkin shape. Soft rind with dense meat. Flavorful, sweet, and nutty. Ideal as an edible serving dish.

SPAGHETTI SQUASH (VEGETABLE SPAGHETTI, ORANGETTI) Yellow watermelon-shaped squash. Developed in Japan. Weighs 2 to 4 pounds. Pale yellow meat separates into strands resembling spaghetti when cooked. Hard rind with mild, nutlike flavor. Not interchangeable with other winter squash. Available year-round.

SUGAR LOAF Dark green stripes over light tan background, cylindrical shape. Developed at the Oregon Agricultural Experiment Station. Related to Delicata. Soft rind with yellow, firm, medium dry meat with large seed cavity. Rich, sweet flavor. Ideal for stuffing.

SWEET DUMPLING (ORIGINALLY CALLED VEGETABLE GOURD) Green stripes over a cream background; skin turns deep orange over yellow as it matures. Scalloped pumpkin shape. Weighs 1 to 1½ pounds. Developed in Japan. Soft rind with pale yellow-orange meat. Smooth and sweet. Good size for stuffing. Does not store well.

TURBAN (TURK'S TURBAN) Brightly colored, usually orange mottled with green and white. Fancifully shaped squash topped with decorative knobs. Soft rind with orange meat. Sweet and moist. Use first as a decoration, then bake it.

YEAR-ROUND SQUASH

CHAYOTE (MIRLITON, CHRISTOPHENE, VEGETABLE PEAR, XUXU) Light to dark green, mostly smooth, but sometimes spiny, skin sometimes ridged lengthwise. Pear-shaped chayote (pronounced cha-OH-tay) is in the genus *Sechium edule*, a cousin to the *Cucurbita* clan. Grown in the tropics of Mexico and Central America, as well as Florida. Popular in Louisiana. Average weight is ¾ pound. Similar to summer squash, but requires longer cooking. The single, flat seed is edible. Mild taste, somewhere between a cucumber and zucchini. Generally available year-round.

Index

Table of Equivalents

The exact equivalents in the following tables have been rounded for convenience.

WEIGHTS

US/UK

oz = *ounce*

lb = *pound*

in = *inch*

ft = *foot*

tbl = *tablespoon*

fl oz = *fluid ounce*

qt = *quart*

US/UK	METRIC
1 oz	30 g
2 oz	60 g
3 oz	90 g
4 oz (¼ lb)	125 g
5 oz (⅓ lb)	155 g
6 oz	185 g
7 oz	220 g
8 oz (½ lb)	250 g
10 oz	315 g
12 oz (¾ lb)	375 g
14 oz	440 g
16 oz (1 lb)	500 g
1 ½ lb	750 g
2 lb	1 kg
3 lb	1.5 kg

METRIC

g = *gram*

kg = *kilogram*

mm = *millimeter*

cm = *centimeter*

ml = *milliliter*

l = *liter*

LIQUIDS

US	METRIC	UK
2 tbl	30 ml	1 fl oz
¼ cup	60 ml	2 fl oz
⅓ cup	80 ml	3 fl oz
½ cup	125 ml	4 fl oz
⅔ cup	160 ml	5 fl oz
¾ cup	180 ml	6 fl oz
1 cup	250 ml	8 fl oz
1 ½ cups	375 ml	12 fl oz
2 cups	500 ml	16 fl oz
4 cups/1 qt	1 liter	32 fl oz

LENGTH MEASURES

⅛ in	3 mm
¼ in	6 mm
½ in	12 mm
1 in	2.5 cm
2 in	5 cm
3 in	7.5 cm
4 in	10 cm
5 in	13 cm
6 in	15 cm
7 in	18 cm
8 in	20 cm
9 in	23 cm
10 in	25 cm
11 in	28 cm
12 in/1 ft	30 cm

OVEN TEMPERATURES

FAHRENHEIT	CELSIUS	GAS
250	120	½
275	140	1
300	150	2
325	160	3
350	180	4
375	190	5
400	200	6
425	220	7
450	230	8
475	240	9
500	260	10

Mother's

www.debbiemumm.com

new seasons™

I carry my mother's love
with me always, like a precious
keepsake kept close to my heart.

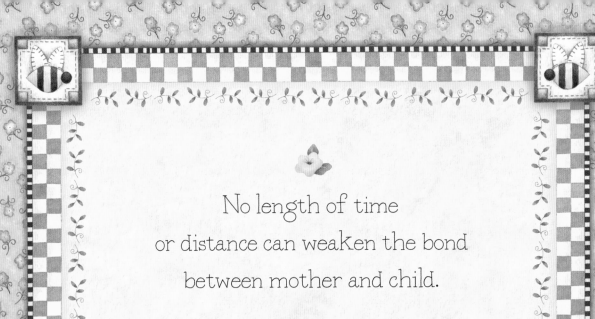

No length of time
or distance can weaken the bond
between mother and child.

An empty nest is a
mother's pride as much as
it is her sorrow.

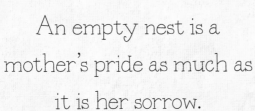

Mothers are the center
of everything in a child's life:
nourishment, comfort, and
always, love.

Sometimes the best thing I can
do as a mother is to remember
what it was like to be a child.

A mother gives birth not just to a child,
but to a greater vision of love and joy
than she could ever hope for herself.

The sweetest
sounds to
mortals given
Are heard
in Mother,
Home, and
Heaven.

-WILLIAM GOLDSMITH BROWN,
MOTHER, HOME, HEAVEN-

If you never
leave your children,
how will they ever
learn that you will
always come back
to them?

BLESS the BIRDS

SONGBIRDS

FLY AWAY HOME

A mother is someone who loves and
supports you as you pursue your dreams.

Most mothers are
instinctive philosophers.

-Harriet Beecher Stowe-

A man may work
from sun to sun,
but woman's work
is never done.

Sometimes it is right to share our wisdom and lead those we love to correct answers. Other times it is far wiser to stand quietly in the shadows, allowing someone dear to stumble upon her own answers.

When love doesn't conquer all,
homemade cookies come close.

Whatever her accomplishments,
a mother measures her success by
the goodness in her children.

The path of motherhood can take unexpected turns. But it is in its twists and turns, its hills and valleys, that we experience new and surprising joys.

Our children learn only what we
teach them. If we allow ourselves to fly, to
dream, and to love, they will do the same.

Every one can keep House better
than her Mother, till she trieth.

-THOMAS FULLER, GNOMOLOGIA-

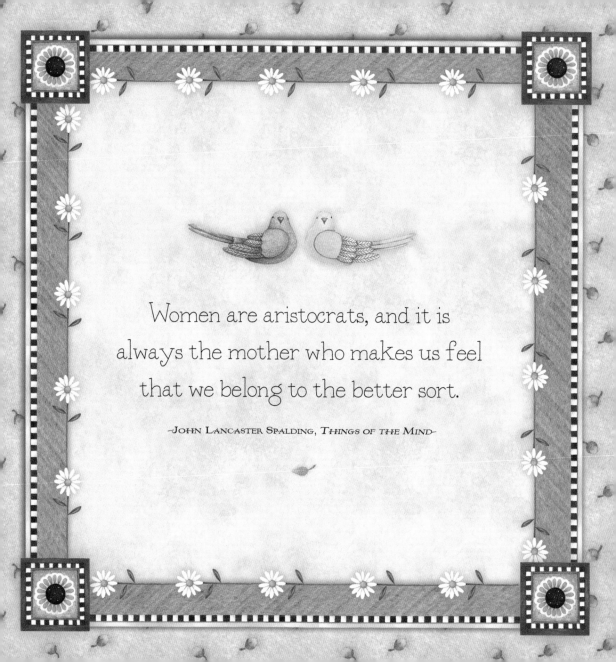

Women are aristocrats, and it is
always the mother who makes us feel
that we belong to the better sort.

-JOHN LANCASTER SPALDING, *THINGS OF THE MIND*-

When a mother follows her own
pursuits and passions, her children
learn to follow theirs.

There was never a child so lovely,
but his mother was glad to get him asleep.

-RALPH WALDO EMERSON-

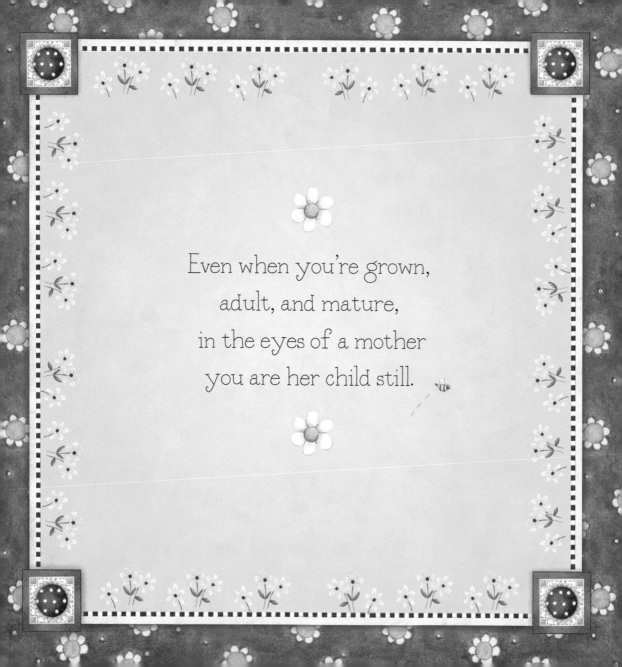

Even when you're grown,
adult, and mature,
in the eyes of a mother
you are her child still.

Mothers are given the greatest
treasure any human can know:
the knowledge that they do make a
difference in someone else's life.

A mother's instinct tells her
when to protect her young;
her intuition tells her when to
let them roam free.

What do girls do
who haven't any mothers
to help them through
their troubles?

-LOUISA MAY ALCOTT-

When will they make measuring spoons in pinches and smidgeons?

Children are children
for a brief time.
Mothers are mothers forever.

COUNTRY
GARDEN

There was never
a great man who
had not a
great mother.

-Olive Schreiner-

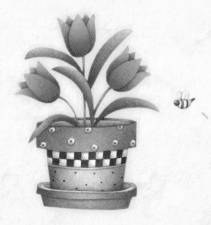

A mother is the heart
of her family; her smile, its beat.

Only a mother knows
a mother's fondness.

-LADY MARY WORTLEY MONTAGU,
IN A LETTER TO THE COUNTESS OF BUTE-

The greatest gifts we can give
our children are unconditional love,
open arms, and a willing ear.

Like a glacier, the first
five years crawl by.
The next ten years
like a jet plane fly.
The last three of childhood,
in the blink of an eye.

Every now and then think
like a grandma instead of a mom.
Let your kids have ice cream for breakfast.
Go ahead and buy that little toy
they want in the supermarket.
Have a good, long cuddle like you
don't see them every day.

Motherhood:

a job with no vacation

or overtime pay~which proves it's

truly a managerial position.

Watch your child's face as she
celebrates life. Learn from your child.
Her lessons are illuminating.

Mother,
strong and sweet,
your gentle voice
brings joy.
Your love
never ceases.

A mother is the
truest friend
we have when trials,
heavy and sudden,
fall upon us;
when adversity
takes the place of
prosperity.

~WASHINGTON IRVING~

Far more inspiring than
watching a movie is watching your
baby teach himself to walk.

One of the most valuable
gifts a mother can give a child
is her good example.

A mother understands
what a child does not say.

—JEWISH PROVERB—

©Debbie Mumm

Cultivate the garden
of your heart and watch love bloom!

A woman better understands
her mother after she becomes one.

My mother's love is the gift of wings
that lets my spirit take flight.

The power of a mother's touch
is nothing short of miraculous.
With one sweep across a weary
forehead, one turn of a wayward curl,
merely mortal fingers can bring
divine peace and blissful slumber.